UNR

Supported using public funding by
ARTS COUNCIL ENGLAND

Supported using public funding by Arts Council England

ISBN:978-1-913642-43-3

Book designed by Aaron Kent

Edited by Aaron Kent

Broken Sleep Books (2021), Talgarreg, Wales

Contents

Unravelanche

Jon Stone

*

The ice pilot leaves her boat, setting out on foot across the pans. This is north of the circle, north of the spit, beyond the final chapter of land as we know it. No epilogue, no afterword, no postscript. Fast ice, then the floes. Pages and pages of white.

She takes with her a sled, a folding field camera, biscuits, tins of pemmican, skis and stove. Lamp, collapsible kayak. Pick. Cocoa. Her course plotted, she walks for three days before unpacking the camera, loading the first plates, exposing them.

East Anglia Shipwrecks

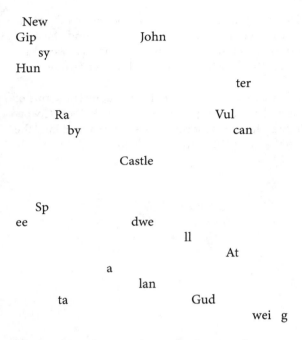

```
New
Gip                    John
    sy
Hun
                                   ter

        Ra                    Vul
          by                    can

              Castle


        Sp
ee                  dwe
                         ll
                                   At
              a
                  lan
        ta              Gud
                              wei  g
```

These were the smacksmen salvagers from
Brightlingsea.   They were close to panic.
              The shock brought them tum-
bling out.

Cat's Cradle

Gre
      en
                        earth

   Blue-
                                  wh
                ite

   pearl
                            the
                                great

door

       of

         heaven.
  AH-
                       WHO
         OM
I looked up at the sky where the bird had been.
It buzzed like bees. It swayed.
We all looked up
            then at one another.

*

This is the outer membrane of the storm, its stray, surly thrusts. Their impression on silver salts in gelatin. These images, when later developed, will prove what the ice pilot already knows: there is a library trapped in the ice.

No, not trapped – fused, overlapped, intermaterialised. And for some time its structural integrity has been weakening. Its edges are being shorn off. Slivers of it carried for miles.

Words from the same text, she sees, retain a powerful attraction to one another, forming sentences as they settle on the ground.

The Ghost with Trembling Wings

gol

      den

toad   har

          le

             quin

    frog

      flam

        boy

ant

  ly

      col

        our

       ed

temp

  orary

           pud

       dles

Imagine a maker of jewellery, conjuring
a bangle in the shape of an amphibian;
      pouring in the hot, molten metal,
burnishing and polishing the cooling cast.

The Mysterious Flame of Queen Loana

Pure

bloo   ded

   Ital
                              ian

                                                Half-
pow

                              dered   face
   Lie
              Voi   Sie

   Anna
                      bella

                          apes
                                        curves
      bony

But beautiful above all else were the images,
in magazines and publicity posters,
                of brash, dishevelled legs,
dark eyes on delicate soldiers.

*

The hullaballoo of the winds increases hour on hour, along with their verbosity. The ice pilot menaces herself with pronouncements. She hates the cold. She hates the thick and greasy pemmican. She is ever on the cusp of becoming lost – fooled by the movement of the drift ice beneath her.

But the library has called to no one else. There are others who are distantly, coolly aware of it, yes, but for them it is enough to know it exists, to conjure its impression every now and then. She alone is compelled to become enveloped in it.

Proverb: *every kind of courage has its corresponding torrent, waiting to swallow it whole.*

His Last Bow

Nine

o'   clock.

Sun

long

set.

The   study.

The

ter

race.

The

lock.

Dust   coat.

Small

blue

book.

The lights of a small car shone vividly into the open safe.
He broke a small key from his watch-chain.
"The sweet old song, it is my ruin forever."

Biggles in the Jungle

Rif
le   Pet
                            rol

tank   Luc
                    ky
                            shot

        Glan
    cing
                    blow   A

    brisk
                fire
A
                        jag
                            ged
        hole
                Pink
    dawn

Then, round a shoulder of rock far below them,
appeared that Tiger, the mounting sun.
Algy emptied his revolver
            into the animal's sleek flank.

The Left Hand of Darkness

Thi

      eves   Fog

            Dusk

Jit

         ters   Cin

                         ders

    soc

        ket   hiss

             wax

ing   moon

     freak

            soot

   sledge

                 peak

Up here the ice shakes less. The lower valley of the glaciers
behind us is white with steam.
Ash and snow, fire and dark.
     A dull red bloom on the belly of night.

Far from the Madding Crowd

Bright

air

Reins

King

fish

er

Low

dress   shires

bonds

wind-

ward

cow

shed

blue

wood-   smoke

knot

of   spar

rows

The sluggish day began to break. The hat
she had lost in the wind, its noiselessness that of a hawk.
A boy bringing a milking-pail,
a bowed sapling.

*

Lying bruisedly in her tent, the ice pilot writes imaginary lines in an imaginary journal. She mulls over the fate of empires: not to disappear leaving the odd broken plinth, but to be gnawed to particles, those particles mixing in flurries and eddies. To become indecipherably woven together with former enemies, with the lowly and left-in-the-dust. To become a faint spray across the star that lights another empire.

Outside the tent, the wind is so loud and so garrulous it seems almost to loop back again into silence. Sinking slow toward morning, the ice pilot is close to convincing herself that the storm is an echo or recollection. That she is in a cabin on a ship, playing it on repeat – as if a twin-spooled tape ran hissing from ear to ear.

Dragonsdawn

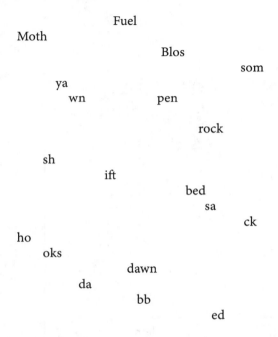

Even the fire-lizards sprawled. The riders
disappeared, skimming the treetops.
Sean held his hand up for silence,
shock-proof in the sea-ivy.

Ice Station Zebra

                                        Haz
                                            ards
oil
            huts
                                    gale-
                                        for
                                                ce
        lamp
                    lips

    whis
                                    ky
            men
                        Doc
                                        Skin
                bulk
        he   ads

                        jet
grip
                                        dam
The ice sloped up sharply to a ghostly
hooped steel skeleton, fire-charred
goggles and snow-masks.
No ridges, no hummocks, no crevasses.

Catching Fire

scarf

                                  bre

                                       ath

blow

            tor   ch

                             clev

                                    er

                fin

            gers

cro

    wn   dart

                                    jaw

ribs

           sha

              kes

                        pang

   bea

      ch

               tick

                        tock

If I feel ragged, very blond in the sunlight,
I blend into the trees.
Is this the way President Snow knows about the kiss?
All I can see
        is trespassing.

Autobots' Lightning Strike

steel

                                             mast

SCRA

       MBLE   spike

             back

  arc

               spark

      scorch

                         Fuses

   blew

             rock

mega

                  volts

     flash

            WOW!

  riven

                clouds

For hours, Soundwave remained on the hilltop.
He tuned his audio sensors to their finest pitch.
The rain fussed on hot metal.
               It will be your undoing.

*

'Undoing'. The ice pilot thinks this an odd term for the end. As if we were each a single, awkward knot tied in the mooring line of a balloon, perhaps. So that when we expire, we release something that is not ourselves.

She has come far enough, she supposes, to be somewhere near the core of it. Deep into a wing at least. Her supply of plates is running low – but the noise is much diminished. The library has howled and howled at her through dinners, report-writing, nights on research and leisure vessels. Now its voice is a gentle croon.

The Virgin and the Gypsy

                    cliff
                        of
                            wa
        ter
                mill   -race
                        whirled

                    Up
            heaved
    spume
                his   sing
                            cold-
            wracked
                wild   wet
                    cap
                        gone
        gap
                    blew   vaga
            bond
                            teeth

But by that time the girls were both hag-eyed,
abstracted, hardly heeding.
    They perched there on the ladder,
year after year, year after year.

The Besieged City

               moving
    eye
                            brows
  pub lic
        in   com pre   hen
                    sion
dancer,
                in   elast
  ic   terrible
noon   mascu
              line   myst
  eri
        ous   so
    much   shy   ness,
Doctor   Light   house
     love
with   bru   tality
      use less   and
    resplen
                        dent

Real rats, famous and unknown, rolled
    into a rainy night, a ballroom, another ballroom.
"Yes, yes," she'd say, weakened by this excess:
        "yes, yes!"

The Observer's Book of Masqueraders

Gather
            ing   satin
                              sti
tch
              godd   ess

        kind   ling
                        mater
        ial
                                              dots
            coxcomb
                              school
      ro   om
            smo   ocked
                  bed

  cape   scal
              loped

                        neck

He unclenched his herringboned hem,
and showed her the crushed letter.
        She dragged one long thread through
his burning mouth.

A Play of Benighted Bodies

     of movem   ent
              manifestat
                  ion
o'erleapt
         dia   chrony

daycast   ver ges
         choirs   of
    gangs ter
                     tongue
  con   fig   ura
               tion   dial
  tac   tics   gifted
    lumi   nous   scho
  lar
       em   wounded
eye   jazz   clim
   ax   pitched   ag   ainst
     serial
         terrest   rial

Here we encounter sacrifice, salt tide:
        the simple layout and minimal semaphore
  of run, jump, talk, exhume. Nothing keeps me
attuned to its capacity.

*

It's twenty-four more hours before she reaches the wall. By now her lip is blackened and split, her finger-ends raw. A few of the nerves in her mouth still dance as she bites into an oat biscuit.

Like Wilde's Salome, "she shows herself naked in the sky", somehow, through her medley of wools. The sky itself is the vastest eye.

And the wall of the library – that nucleus which has not yet been whipped into debris – is so tall that the whiteness of its peak merges with the white of that great eye. Its surface is made of layer upon layer of darkly luminous script, encased. Like miniscule cracks in a glass that is ready to shatter.

The slightest touch will incinerate her.

The Woman in Drēama

wornas   widsceope
          Ah,   de   ar!
    bi   noman   hāten   best
                        ānsta   gra
                              pan   ce
    dare   say   gemet fæst
        lufsum   with   out
u   tte   ri   ng
                    a
                        word   wlitig
    and   wynsum   trif
                                                            les

        hand
                kerch
                            ief   cynes
                                        tōlum
        spy

This was the Secret, and it was
her fyrngeflitan. Swēttra and swīþra, that last misty
death-swoon. Scattered over the table.
                        Swā bið scinnena þēaw.

The World of Perception

dual   char   crow
                       acteris
                                    ics   that
thus
              'twas   bade   anal
                                                    ysis
     sign'd   with
              en dear   vour
     Muse   ums
              Ay,   t'amal
                                                    game
mercu   ry   ,
                              uni   on
     rights   pewter
                   class   ical
     tricks   o'
              the   cards   duc
tile   cus   toms
        broths
                                                    chalk
     clay   wheels

Let us now turn from our fat ram-vellum
     to see what becomes of these blear'd eyes,
the plumed coherence.
This temptation is particularly strong.

Acknowledgements

I made the snowstorm poems (or 'snowems') originally for close friends and family, back in 2015, as Christmas cards. I had a different person in mind for each text I selected, so collectively this merry band are the main inspiration behind the sequence. The source texts themselves are acknowledged in/as the poem's titles. I think it's more fun if I leave it to you to track down the authors and publishers, if you are so inclined.

My thanks to Aaron Kent for his generosity and enthusiasm in taking on a strange and shivery little book, and to Kirsten Irving for her perceptive editorial suggestions.

LAY OUT YOUR UNREST